To the amazing Ms. Snow & he

"Yippee!"

Someday
I'll be a
Teacher

2015

Someday I'll be a Teacher

60 Kid-Voiced Verses That Celebrate Teachers and School

by Ted Scheu
Photographs by Peter Lourie

Young Poets' Press

MIDDLEBURY, VT

Very special thanks to a cool bunch of camera-stars
at the Rutland Town School, in Rutland, VT, and
their dedicated teachers, parents, and principal.
You guys are the best!

Huge thanks to our awesome 'production team':
my endlessly-supportive wife, Robin; my sharp-eyed,
open-hearted editor, Angie Wiechmann;
my always-inspiring friend and awesome photo-
grapher, Pete Lourie; and the brilliantly-creative
Win Colwell, my designer and friend.

Someday I'll be a Teacher
First Edition, April 2015

Text copyright © 2015 by Ted Scheu
Photographs copyright © 2015 by Peter Lourie
Design by Winslow Colwell/WrenSong Design

Published in the United States by Young Poets' Press
www.youngpoetspress.com

For further information, or to reproduce selections from this book, write to
Young Poets' Press
PO Box 564, Middlebury, VT 05753

The text of this publication was set in American Typewriter.
ISBN 978-0-9825499-6-4

Library of Congress Control Number: 2014913992

THIS COLLECTION IS DEDICATED, WITH GREAT
THANKS, ADMIRATION AND AWE TO ALL
THE DEEPLY-COMMITTED AND CREATIVE
TEACHERS ON THE PLANET
- MANY OF WHOM I HAVE HAD THE
GREAT HONOR OF WORKING WITH -
WHO MAKE A DIFFERENCE IN THE LIVES
OF CHILDREN EACH DAY.

Table of Contents

Someday I'll Be a Teacher

When I grow up, I think I'll be
a teacher at my school.
I'll be the kind that kids will find
to be extremely cool.

I've watched my teachers carefully.
I've seen the stuff they do.
And I'm completely confident
that I could do it too.

I'm super great at helping kids,
like teachers do all day.
And all the things they say to us
are things that I can say.

I'm smart enough to answer kids
whenever they don't know stuff.
And I'd be sure the kids I'd teach
would never try to throw stuff.

I like to chat with grownups.
I'm great at writing notes.
I'm awesome cleaning sinks and floors
and hanging winter coats.

I would not sleep at meetings
and never would be mean.
And I'm the best of all my friends
at keeping whiteboards clean.

I know I have the skills I need
to do it easily.
And I'll be sure the kids I teach
are perfect—just like me!

Who Needs Recess?

They took our recess time away
so we can study more.
We practice stuff that's on the tests
to get a higher score.

We barely even stop for snack—
there isn't time to do it.
We've got important work to do
and need to hurry through it.

Besides, who needs a recess break?
Who needs to jump and run?
To be as smart as we can be,
who needs to see the sun?

Who needs to play a silly game?
Who needs to breathe fresh air?
Who needs to feel the wild wind
whooshing through his hair?

I need to get my highest score,
and I will always try to.
So, who needs recess anyway?

I'm pretty sure that I do.

Today

Today I am the sharpest kid
the world has ever known.
I'm wicked hot and super cool—
completely "in the zone."

Today I know that I could leap
the tallest mountain peak.
And I could swim around the world
in just about a week.

Today I'm feeling faster
than a cheetah chasing dinner.
And if I ran for president,
I know I'd be the winner.

Today my brain is brighter
than a beam of laser light.
My heart is soaring higher
than a wild flying kite.

Today I even might recite
a billion books by heart.
And all because my teacher stopped
and told me I was smart.

I Tickled My Teachers

I tickled each of my teachers today;
you should have seen their eyes.
I never thought a teacher's face
could show so much surprise.

Tickling teachers is usually
a dangerous thing to do.
But when you hear how well it worked,
you'll want to try it too.

It doesn't take a special skill,
but prob'ly you should know
I never used my finger,
and I never touched a toe.

Instead, I said, "good morning"
as I slid into my seat.
And when we wrote, I strained to make
my letters extra neat.

I raised my hand politely,
and I didn't stomp or yell.
I kept my snake inside its box
at morning show-and-tell.

I took my turn at recess,
and I never slid in mud.
I didn't spill the ketchup
and pretend that it was blood.

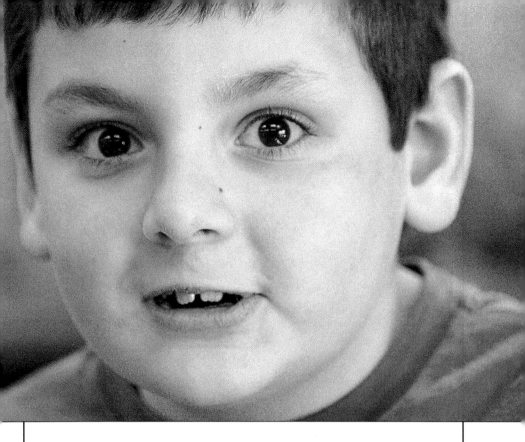

I didn't push a single kid
or cut a single line.
And when I didn't get my way,
I almost didn't whine.

This sounds a little crazy,
but it's absolutely true.
My teachers all were smiling
by the time the day was through.

But tickling teachers is tiring, too,
and harder than I thought.
So will I tickle tomorrow again?
Absolutely! (Not!)

Parent-Teacher Conference

My homework's always overdue—
it makes my teacher mad.
So, she arranged a conference
with me and Mom and Dad.

I know she wants to ask them
why I procrastinate.
But she may never get the chance—
my parents both are late.

A Better Report Card

I dragged my new report card home;
it seemed to weigh a ton.
"Next time," my parents growled at me,
"bring back a better one."

So, when our grades arrive next time,
I'll really use my head.
I'll borrow a card from my smartest friend
and bring hers home instead.

I'm Staying Here

I have a brief announcement—
I'd like to make it clear:
I'm staying here in second grade
for more than just this year.

I love it here, I'm pleased to say.
And though it may sound strange,
I know inside I've hit my stride,
and I don't need to change.

My teacher's style makes me smile—
she's strict, but kind and funny.
So, I will *never* leave this place.
I'm like a bear with honey.

There's awesome science stuff to do
and books I love to read.
The writing is exciting,
and the math is just my speed.

Besides, those bossy third-grade kids
are way too big and tough.
I saw them out at recess,
and they play a little rough.

Hooray, hooray for second grade!
I need to shout and cheer!
It's cool to think in twenty years
that I will still be here.

I Like the Me I See

I like the me I see today—
the way my smile fits.
And I'm inclined to trust the way
my body stands and sits.

I like my hair and how it hangs
to frame my eager face.
And even, I suppose, my nose
does not seem out of place.

I like the me I see today—
the way my shoulders rise.
And I can very clearly see
a twinkle in my eyes.

They watch the world more carefully
than they have done before.
And all my other senses too
are "seeing" so much more.

I'm feeling fairly satisfied
with how I hold my hands.
My body seems agreeable
to follow my commands.

I like the me I see today—
from tippy-top to toes.
And here's the most amazing thing—
I even like my clothes!

Today my body seems to fit
the size it's meant to be.
It makes me stop and wonder
if this is really *me*!

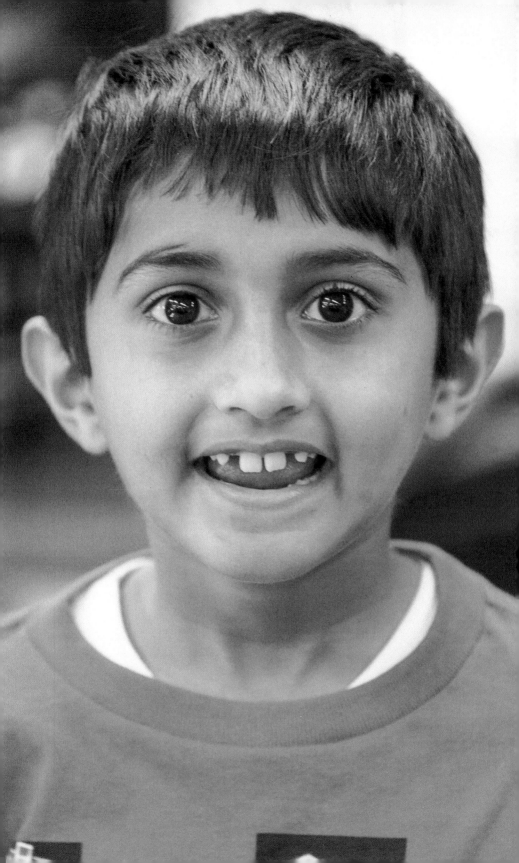

Don't Call My Teacher "Nice"

Don't *ever* call my teacher "nice."
She doesn't quite deserve it.
Come in someday and watch her work,
and we can both observe it.

"Nice" will never work for her,
when better words will do.
In fact, I've made a list right here
of more than just a few.

She isn't nice—she's fabulous
and marvelous and great.
She's totally incredible,
as she will demonstrate.

Her manner is stupendous.
She's quick and kind and smart.
She makes us feel like we're the best
at everything we start.

So, please don't ever call her "nice"—
the word is dull and flat.
She's just the super-est teacher there is,
and *that* is simply *that*.

Cursive Curse

My *m*s are much too bumpy.
My *u*s are far too lumpy.
My *k*s are way too droopy.
My *l*s are all too loopy.
My *e*s are *i*s, and *i*s are *e*s.
My *z*s have got some rare disease.
My tails are tilted to the right.
My *x* is not a handsome sight.
My wimpy *r*s are worst of all;
the bumps on top are much too small.

My pencil shouts to stop for air.
My hand is sore—this isn't fair.
My teacher doesn't understand.
I'll *never* have a steady hand.
I feel a need to scream—or worse.
So, close your ears, or you may hear
a bumpy, lumpy, droopy, loopy,
wimpy, skimpy, cursive curse.

Fred and Me
(and My Very Confused Teacher)

"Fred and me got ice cream!" I told my teacher.

"Fred and *I* got ice cream," she said.

"You and Fred got ice cream *too*?"

"No, *you and Fred* got ice cream.'"

"That's what I said."

"No, you said, 'Fred and *me* got ice cream.'

"No. I said, Fred and *I* got ice cream. Not you."

"Good! That's right!"

"I know that's right. I was there. You weren't."

"Look," she said.

I looked. But I didn't see Fred or ice cream or *anything* but her.

"Would you ever say, '*me* got ice cream'?"

"Of course not! That would sound silly."

"Okay. So it will always be, '*Fred and I* got ice cream.' Or you could switch it around and say, 'I got ice cream for *me and Fred...*'"

"You did? Fred didn't tell me he got ice cream with you *twice!*"

"...So, if you aren't sure whether to say, '*Fred and me*' or '*Fred and I,*' then just leave Fred off. You'll know. It'll sound right."

That didn't sound right to me at all.

I'd *never* leave Fred off.

We're best friends.

Teachers sure can be *confused* sometimes.

Twice More

I have two ears to hear the world,
and two fine eyes to read it.
I also have one tender tongue,
in case it's ever needed.

From watching teachers, I have learned
(although I'm still quite young),
it's best to use my ears and eyes
twice more than my tongue.

The Most Embarrassing Three-Letter Word to Ever Utter in a Quiet Classroom

My brain is wobbling wildly.
My face is blooming red.
I'd pay a billion dollars
to unsay what I just said.

The teasing is increasing
as I struggle to stay calm.
I don't know why my tongue and I
just called my teacher "Mom."

Testing, Testing, Testing!

Testing, testing, testing!
They're testing us to death.
At school, we take so many tests
we're almost out of breath...

From testing, testing, testing!
It's all we seem to do.
If you could look inside our brains
you'd see they're black and blue...

From testing, testing, testing!
And that is my concern.
We take so many tests each week,
there's barely time to *learn*.

Smarter Than Martin

I'm not as smart as Martin
when it comes to multiplying.
I'll never be the whiz he is
in science, but I'm trying.

Martin's mind is quicker
when we have to memorize.
I'm pretty sure my brain for that
is just a different size.

I'm not as calm and confident
at sharing book reports.
Martin's words are thunderstorms,
and mine are squeaky snorts.

Even writing poems,
he's funnier and quicker.
Martin's rhymes get claps and laughs,
and mine might get a snicker.

We're also very different
with books that we are reading.
I slither like a sleepy slug,
while Martin's always speeding.

But when it comes to climbing ropes
and running fast in gym,
he knows that I will always be
way smarter than him.

Memory Aid

My memory is horrible—
I never have a clue.
I can't remember when or where
or what or why or who.

My teacher had a great idea:
a notebook where I write
the stuff I need to focus on
for homework every night.

So, now I will be ready
for every test and quiz—
if only I'd remember where
my stupid notebook is.

Teaching My Teacher

I've never been the best in math—
my "calculator's" slow.
But I could not believe the things
my *teacher* didn't know.

She asked if I could show her how
to count to ninety-eight.
And then I read the calendar
and figured out the date.

I showed her, in a number,
where the tens and hundreds go,
and all she did was shake her head
and blankly whisper, "Oh."

She didn't know the value
of a dollar and a cent.
And then I had to demonstrate
what *"odd"* and *"even"* meant.

I showed her how to measure
with a ruler and a scale
and how to predict, if coins are flipped,
if it's a head or tail.

The clock was next—she didn't seem
to know about the hands.
But now, because I taught her well,
I think she understands.

We added up some numbers,
and did some take-aways.
She finally seemed to get it,
so I showered her with praise.

I told her it was fun to be
her teacher for the day,
and since she'd worked so hard,
I said to "take a break and play."

Despite the noisy classroom,
she'd performed extremely well.
I urged her not to worry,
and I promised not to tell.

I said that "every brain has got
a different learning speed."
Maybe tomorrow I'll teach her how
to spell and write and read.

I Adore the Common Core

I just adore the Common Core.
It meets my needs precisely.
Since I'm a kid who loves to learn,
it fits my style nicely.

It tells me what I have to know
and when I need to know it.
I meet a standard at my pace
then get a chance to show it.

The Core and I are BFFs—
like butter on our bread.
I even read it every night
before I go to bed.

It's better than a storybook—
much more complete and deep.
And since it's pretty boring too
it puts me right to sleep.

The Common Core is great for me.
I'm glad they chose to choose it.
And maybe, someday, they will teach
our teachers how to use it.

I'm Having a Grumpy Day

Excuse me, but I need to say,
I'm having quite a grumpy day.
The clouds above seem extra ashen,
and grins are clearly out of fashion.
But I will grit my teeth and try
to move the oceans, land, and sky.
My grumpy mood may not agree,
but all those eager faces,
determined, in their places,
are counting on their teacher—me.

Summer School Is Awesome

I know it sounds ridiculous
and opposite of cool,
but summer is my favorite time
to hang around my school.

I get my choice of classrooms,
and any desk is *mine*.
And finally the water fountain
doesn't have a line.

Since no one's there to catch me,
I race around the halls.
And on the playground, I don't share
the swings or bouncy balls.

I get to go to specials
anytime I'm bored.
And every great idea I have
is totally adored.

The quiet helps me concentrate.
My brain stays calm and clear.
And I remember all the stuff
I should have learned last year.

I love to come to summer school,
when life is fun and full.
It's totally the greatest time
to be the principal.

I Call First

"I call first to get a drink! And first to eat my snack!"
"I call first to go to gym, and first when we come back!"

"I call first to leave for lunch! And first to switch the light!"
"I call first to read out loud the poems that I write!"

"I call first to sharpen up my pencil, loud and slow!"
"And when we get to sharing time, I call first to show!"

"I call the computer! I get the special chair!"
"And I call first in line each time that we go anywhere!"

"And on the hill at recess, I get to be the king!"
"I call first forever and for every little thing!"

I said those things in class today,
until my teacher heard.
She sat right down and made a list
to keep me at my word.

So now I'm first to dump the trash,
and sweep the sticky floors.
I'm first to be the last in line
'cause I hold *all* the doors.

I'm first to wipe the tables off
and scrape off clods of clay.
I'm first to pass the paper out
and put the paints away.

I'm first to stack the silly chairs
and first to scrub the sink.
I'm prob'ly not the first to see
that being first can *stink*!

Someone Who Resembles Me

There's someone who resembles me
who came to school this year.
The other me you used to know
has found a new career.

I'm pretty sure you'll be impressed
with what this new kid shares.
And notice how his body fits
much better in the chairs.

Unlike my hands, the new boy's hands
are brave and rarely tremble.
So, please feel free to call on him—
the kid whom I resemble.

I met the boy at summer camp
and really liked his style.
He taught me how to lose and win
and through it all to smile.

The me you knew has been replaced
by someone even smarter.
Although I did okay last year,
this new kid works much harder.

He's thrilled to be in school for me
and says he loves to learn.
Don't be surprised if last year's me
decides he won't return.

Arithmetic Friends

I'm sorry you are hurting so
and feeling sick and sad.
I wish inside my head I'd find
some words that I could add.

I'm feeling awfully awkward.
I'm not sure how to act.
I wish I had a magic wand
to make your pain subtract.

I hurt when you're unhappy.
I cringe to see you cry.
I'd love to find a tiny smile
and make it multiply.

I'll stay until we find one,
on that I am decided.
'Cause we're the kind of friends
that cannot ever be divided.

I Predict

Our teacher stops our story time
and asks us to predict.
I try to guess what's coming next,
and sometimes I get picked.

I'm pretty good at doing it,
and often I am right.
Like, I predict that later on
today will be tonight.

I predict that two plus two
will always equal four.
And I'm completely confident
my dad will always snore.

I predict the sun will rise
and winter will bring ice.
And I predict, for my whole life,
my brother won't be nice.

I predict that stars will shine
and milk will come from cows.
And I predict, with certainty,
this poem will end right now.

Disappointment

The bouncy balls are waiting
in their basket by the door.
The jump ropes lurk like eager snakes
in coils on the floor.

A box of cones and bases
is sitting patiently,
and coats and outdoor voices
are longing to be free.

Above it all, a cloud has formed
that's deep and dark and wide.
The principal has just announced
that recess is *inside*.

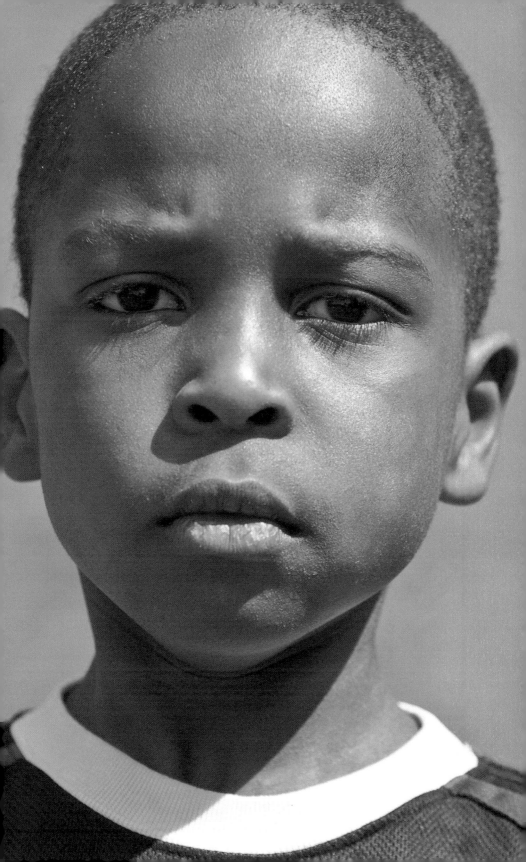

My Parents Are Pretending

I'm pretty sure my parents are
pretending they are sick.
I know because I taught them both
to do that little trick.

You blow your nose, and hold your head
and claim your brain is breaking.
And so, a pro like me would know
my folks are clearly faking.

A little thing I learned in school
convinced me I am right.
My parents are supposed to meet
my principal tonight.

My Teacher Called

My teacher called me just to say
the class was missing me today.

She wished that I would come back quick
and hoped I wasn't feeling sick.

I also noticed nervously
that she was sounding mad at me.

She said I'd missed a spelling test,
and clearly she was nearly stressed.

I thanked her kindly for her call,
then flushed and hurried down the hall.

I neatly hung the bathroom pass
and took my seat behind the class.

I think tomorrow I'll be cool
and will not bring my phone to school.

I Got a Hundred Points

In school, I got a *hundred* points
for being extra nice.
And then I got a *hundred* more
for being nice twice.

At snack, I got a *thousand*,
but I did not relax.
By lunch, I had a *million* more
for many thoughtful acts.

When I got home, I told my mom,
and she was quite excited.
So, who awarded all those points?
I'm pleased to say that *I* did!

Dear Mom and Dad

(My Open House Night Letter
I'm Leaving on My Desk Just for You)

I'm glad you've come to school tonight
to see what I've been doing.
As you can tell, it hasn't been
just coloring and gluing.

To save you time, I've made a list
of things you need to know.
There's awesome stuff to do and see
before you have to go.

My family biography
is hanging in the hall.
And please don't miss my pumpkin poem
glowing on the wall.

Our guinea pig is Thelma.
The fish is named Louise.
And don't forget to cover up
your every cough or sneeze.

Be sure to flush and wash with soap,
and always raise your hand
if anything you hear tonight
is hard to understand.

Always use your inside voice
and clean up all your messes.
I want your best on every test,
and fewer "nos" than "yeses."

Please wait your turn on recess swings
and ask for help with laces,
and never, ever cut a line,
or hold your buddies' places.

I guess that's all I need to share—
you'll figure out the rest.
I hope I learn tomorrow
that you both did your best.

Teacher Appreciation Week

It's Teacher Appreciation Week—
a time to launch a cheer
for all the fun, amazing stuff
we've learned with them this year.

We've showered them with chocolates
and flowers by the bunches,
and all our moms are thanking them
with extra-yummy lunches.

Our hands are stained with marker ink
from making cards and signs.
For once, on mine, I even kept
my words between the lines.

I guess our teachers do deserve
this week of thanks and fuss.
Now, I can't wait to celebrate
the week when they thank *us*.

My Strange Class

I don't like *him*;
he's too tall.
She's too bossy.
He's too small.
She looks funny.
He can't walk.
With *her* accent,
she can't talk.
That boy's clothes
are really weird.
Hers are old,
all torn and smeared.
He eats stuff
I'd never touch.
I don't like
her haircut much.
He can't read right.
She can't add.
If *he* stayed home,
then *I'd* be glad.
She's got very
scary eyes.

He smells bad,
and *she* tells lies.
He's too loud,
and *she's* too brainy.
He and *she* are
too complainy.
He's a wimp
at playground games.
Those girls have
the dumbest names.

I'm the only *normal* kid
in my entire school.
No one is as quick and kind,
or quite so smart and cool.

My class is made of *losers*
whose weirdness never ends.
Can *you* believe it?
They don't even want to be my *friends*!

Why My Teacher Is Wrong When She Says That Tomorrow, September 21, Is the Last Day of Summer

Tomorrow is
the start of fall—
that's a fact I know.

But summer stopped
when school began
twenty days ago.

How Can I Be Quiet?

They're taking tests upstairs today,
so, downstairs, we must walk
as silently as sleepy slugs
and whisper when we talk.

But I can hardly keep inside
my happiness and glee.
I want to scream and share my joy
that they aren't testing me.

A Kiss in Class

I kissed a girl in class today,
and, wow, was she surprised.
Her mouth turned even rounder
than the marbles of her eyes.

I thought her cheek would like my kiss,
but that was not the case.
A perfect pink-then-purple pool
began to fill her face.

I learned a painful lesson,
and you had better know it.
If you love your teacher,
find other ways to show it.

I Made Some Great Connections

Each day in school, I try to make
a bunch of great connections.
It's way more fun than doing tests
or spelling-word corrections.

Like, when I read a book on cows,
I thought of cool ice cream.
And when I thought of Brussels sprouts,
I thought that I might scream.

Of course, my strong connecting brain
came up with many others.
When someone mentioned stinky cheese,
I thought about my brothers.

In math, we studied triangles,
and pizza came to mind.
A square became a brownie—
the double-chocolate kind.

Some circles made me quickly think
of burgers on a plate.
From that point on, connections stopped—
I couldn't concentrate.

The hungry train inside my brain
had driven off the track.
Next time I'll save connecting things
till after I've had snack.

I'm Extremely Bright

My sweater is electric orange.
My pants are gleaming green.
And I have got a yellow belt
that's glowing, in between.

My baseball cap is flaming red,
with stripes of pinks and whites.
And on my feet, my sneakers flash
with blinding, blinking lights.

My socks both glow and glisten
with dazzling surprise.
I keep them mostly out of sight
so they won't hurt your eyes.

My teacher complimented me,
and I know she is right.
Today she turned to me and said
that I'm extremely bright.

My Hot-Rod Teacher

I watched my teacher in her car
as she was leaving school.
The car she drives has racing stripes
and lots of shiny, silver pipes.
So while I've known that she is nice,
today I learned she's cool.

Her car made loud and growly sounds
like TV racers' do.
And when she peeled right out of there,
and smoke and rubber filled the air,
I bet the cop who stopped her
thought she was awesome too.

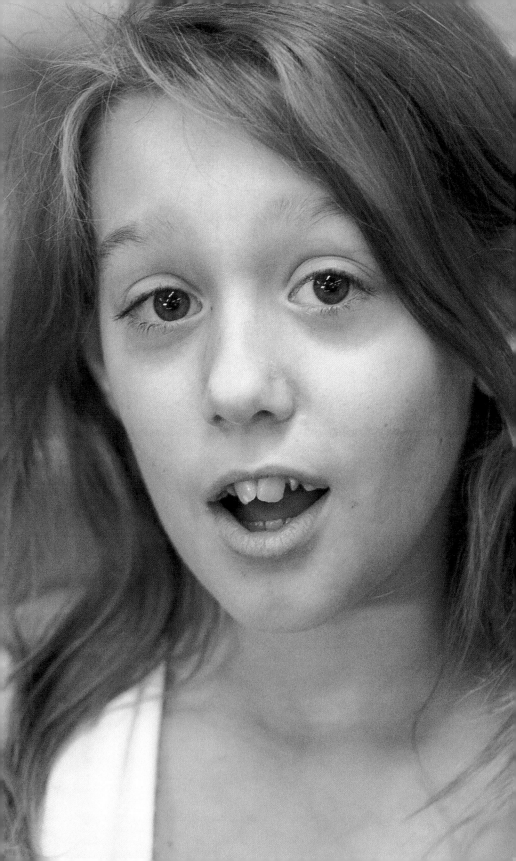

Science Un-Fair

Our science fair was held tonight—
I know the guy who won.
The judges were surprised to see
the work that he had done.

I helped him out a teeny bit,
but it was his design.
I liked that he decided to
include me on his sign.

The crowd could not believe it when
we rolled his gizmo in.
Their eyes were wide in shocked surprise.
All he could do was grin.

The thing began to buzz and blink,
and smoke began to spew.
It's still a mystery to me
the things that thing could do.

It's true his project was the best,
but still, my friends were mad
when all the teachers turned and gave
the trophy to my dad.

Sharing My Gifts

In school today, my teacher said
that I have "great potential."
She said that "sharing all my gifts"
is "totally essential."

I don't know what "potential" is,
but I am glad I've got it.
And when "essential" stuff arrives,
I probably will spot it.

But I am most concerned about
those gifts she says I've got.
I usually find my presents fast,
but this time I cannot.

I'll keep on looking carefully,
although I'm well past caring.
And if I ever find those gifts,
you bet I won't be sharing.

Dear Teacher,

I had the *best* excuse today
explaining clearly why
I couldn't do my homework—
a *perfect* alibi.

The note was neatly written
in my mother's careful hand.
I won't reveal the things it said—
I know you'd understand.

It was the best excuse *by far*—
I won't exaggerate it.
I'd love to show it now to you,
but my stupid puppy ate it.

Come On In!

My school may be the friendliest
of any on the planet.
And I would guess it's been that way
since somebody began it.

You get the warmest welcome
each day as you arrive.
I feel like I'm a happy bee
returning to my hive.

Your ears and eyes catch heaps of "Hi!"
as you fly through the door.
Your spirits start to spread their wings
and leap and swoop and soar.

The sign says "Elementary School,"
but everyone should know
a very friendly "Hi!" school
is where I really go.

High-Tech Teacher

We've got an awesome classroom—
it's all computerized
with all the coolest high-tech stuff
that ever was devised.

We do our lessons on our screens
then click as we get done.
We're learning more than ever now,
and having tons of fun.

And here's the funnest part of all—
we do it on our *own*.
Our teacher stays at home each day
and calls us on the phone.

Apo'strophe's

I never quite remember where
apo'strophe's 'should go.
My teacher alway's roll's her eye's
and tell's me, "You 'should know!"

When Im 'sure I under'stand,
I alway's do it wrong.
And looking up the rule in book's
ju'st take's me way too long.

It's all about po's'se's'sion,
but that i's too confu'sing.
'So I de'signed a 'special trick
you 'see that Ive been u'sing.

I never need to take a chance,
and never have to gue's's.
I drop in one apo'strophe
in front of every 's!

Help Me, Please!

Help me, please,
my knees are jiggling.
All my friends
around are giggling.
Everywhere
my skin is sweating.
Confidence
is fast forgetting.
Need to keep
my hands from shaking.
Not to mention,
stomach quaking.
Eyes are glazy.
Heart is pounding.
Lips are very
funny sounding.
Throat is drying.
Brain is spinning.
I am trying,
but not winning.

This shouldn't be so hard, and yet
it always feels the same.
I *hate* correcting teachers
when they mispronounce my name.

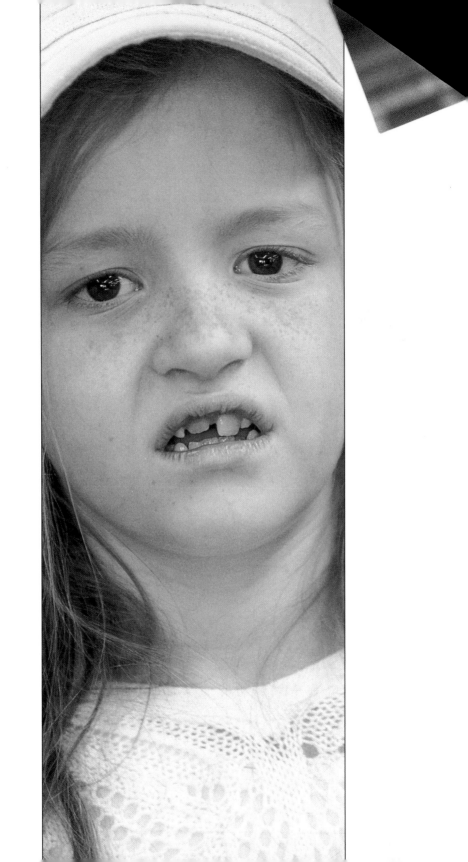

One Out of Two

My teacher says she likes me lots,
so I am feeling glad.
I'd hate to think that being *me*
would make a teacher sad.

The second thing my teacher said
is my *behavior* stinks.
So now I'm quite confused about
the way my teacher thinks.

She likes me as a *person*,
but my *actions* make her mad?
Well, as my parents sometimes say,
"One out of two ain't bad."

We Speak Friend

A new kid joined our class today.
He talks in Japanese.
Another boy speaks Arabic,
with different ABCs.

Two sets of twins speak Spanish,
with words that float like feathers.
It sounds to me like harmony
when they are all together.

I'm fairly sure a Chinese girl
just asked if she could play.
But none of us could understand
the words she had to say.

Although we didn't talk a lot,
we had a bunch of fun.
We raced and ran, without a plan,
beneath the recess sun.

When we all meet tomorrow,
I know we can depend
that we will all communicate
by simply speaking Friend.

How You Can Be as Smart as Me

I love learning,
yes sirree.
I know that one plus one
makes *three*!

Hey, I'm the smartest
kid alive.
I'm sure that two and two
is *five*!

Subtracting's also
lots of fun.
If you take two from four
it's *one*!

In spelling, too,
I am a star.
I see that *c-a-t*
spells *car*!

My brain's the brightest
I have found.
The squares I draw
are extra *round*!

You may not think
this stuff is true.
It is, and here's
what you can do:

If you play video games all day,
and also watch TV,
someday, with lots of work and luck,
you'll be as smart as me!

Our Hundredth Day

Today's our hundredth day of school,
and I could hardly wait
to share the hundred things I brought
to help us celebrate.

I had a hundred jelly beans
of every brilliant hue,
but on the bus they looked so good,
I sort of ate a few.

My hundred yummy chocolate drops
were just a great success—
until they melted in my pants
to make one chocolate mess.

My back up was some cheesy chips
from our convenience store.
But then my brother sat on them
and made two thousand more.

Through my tears, I somehow found
the perfect thing to share:
a hundred short and soggy sobs
came floating through the air.

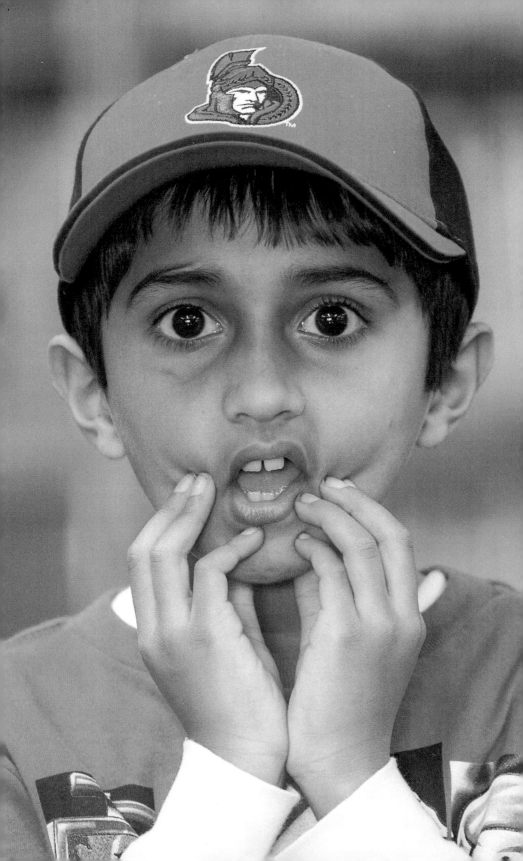

Now I Understand Perfectly

My teacher gave directions.
I raised a quiet hand.
I told her, in a nervous voice,
I didn't understand.

So she repeated everything
the same, but slow and loud.
But all the stuff she said to me
was still a foggy cloud.

I asked again; this time she *yelled*—
her face got stiff and redder.
I don't know why some people think
that louder makes it better.

I gave my brain directions then
I knew were crystal clear:
Do not put up my hand again
until sometime next year.

Look Smart

I have a super-secret trick
that I can share with you.
I've only just discovered it,
so it's completely new.

I keep it just for special friends—
maybe one or two.
Just smile and nod, so teachers think
you know more than you do!

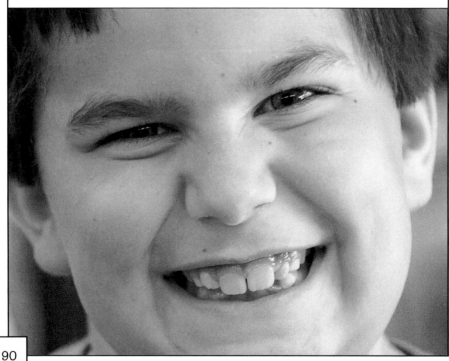

The Weekend Is Coming

The weekend is coming.
I'm counting it down.
The mouth on my face is
no longer a frown.

The weekend is coming.
I'm feeling it's true.
I noticed my teacher
is smiling too.

The weekend is coming
in less than a minute...
and soon... it's a second...
and now...I am in it!

Best Teacher Ever

My teacher, I've decided,
is the best I've ever had.
Of all the things she does in class,
there's *nothing* that is bad.

Okay, there's too much homework,
and rules are wicked strict.
And life will get much harder
in the future, I predict.

She makes us do a couple drafts
of everything we write.
It has to be in *cursive*—
that's not a pretty sight.

With all this stuff, it may sound rough,
and I agree, it can be.
But through it all, I'm glad to say
my teacher understands me.

The reason why I know this fact
may come as quite a shock.
I've noticed that my teacher
always listens when I talk!

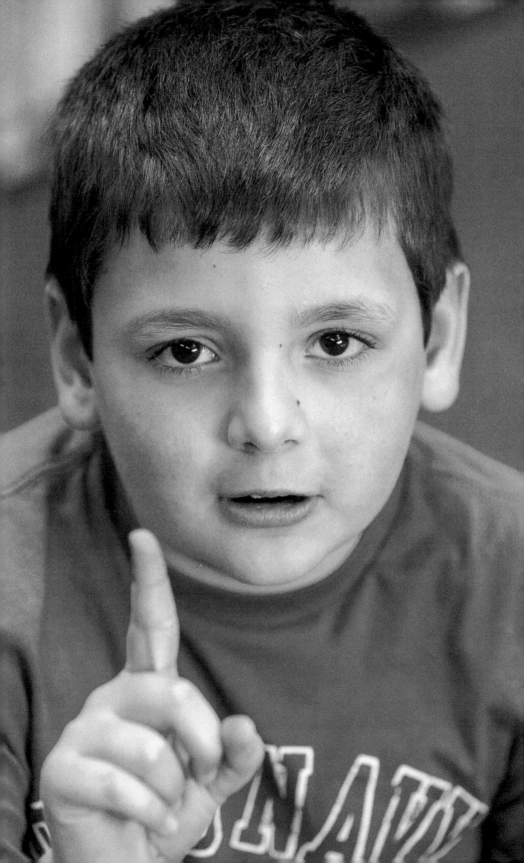

Responsibility Month Is Done

In school we have one special month
when all of us must be
the champs of "best behavior"
and "responsibility."

The more I am reminded, though,
the less I seem to do it.
My mouth and hands don't understand
they need to just get through it.

I try my best. I *really* do.
But I can't play that game.
Trouble seems, for one whole month,
to be my middle name.

So now that March is finally here,
my homework's getting done.
When someone needs a helping hand,
my hand is the one.

I rarely run or cut a line.
I'm causing fewer messes.
Instead of making math mistakes,
I'm adding up successes.

So please don't tell me how to act,
and you will quickly see
I'm so much more responsible
when I don't have to be.

Our Teacher is Totally Tired Today

Our teacher is totally tired today.
We see it in her face,
and how her body sits and stands
and moves from place to place.

Her smile's there, as always,
but even that seems slow.
And twinkles in her teacher-eyes
have lost their sparky glow.

The class is feeling droopy, too,
although we try our best
to do our tip-top work for her
on every quiz and test.

She's tired of the stress, I guess,
and all the testing fuss.
I only hope, when she goes home,
she isn't tired of us.

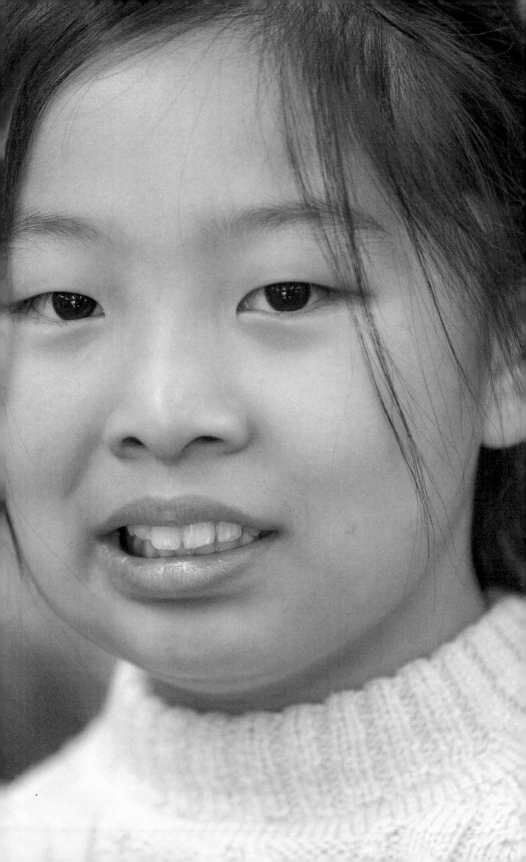

I'm Not a Straight Line Kid

I'll never be a straight line kid,
no matter how I try.
My body needs to twist and turn
and flip and flop and fly.

When we march off to art or gym
along the polished halls,
I spend my time while I'm in line
careening off the walls.

If there is room for me to zoom,
I'll move into a space.
Some toes are fine in quiet lines,
but mine decide to race.

I snake along the corridor
in curvy curlicues.
My path resembles helicopters
flown by kangaroos.

From head to toe I feel as though
I'm swooping through the sky.
While other kids may walk or run,
my feet prefer to fly.

I hope someday my teachers see
and even celebrate
that I will never be inclined
to ever travel straight.

I Fell Awake in Class Today

I fell awake in class today—
my eyes refused to close.
How I got so energized,
heaven only knows.

I tried my very best to sleep,
like always, during writing.
Even yawning wouldn't work—
the class was too exciting.

I begged my brain to take a break
and sneak a quick vacation.
But something in my teacher's voice
encouraged concentration.

I fell awake in class today
and, somehow, did my best.
I hope tomorrow I'll find a way
to get a little rest.

Cooperation's Great!

I've learned cooperation
is really pretty cool.
It's how we do things in our class,
and everywhere at school.

No single kid can whine and pout,
or always have his way.
We find when we cooperate,
it makes a smoother day.

Like, if at quiet reading time,
I want the comfy chair,
then all I do is ask my friends,
and usually they share.

If you would like a crayon of mine—
like plum or midnight blue—
before I'm done, I'll break that one
and give a half to you.

If you get mad and grab it,
because you couldn't wait,
then I'll do something mean to you.
Cooperation's great!

If we decide to have a fight,
then I'll cooperate.
When you whack me, I'll whack you back,
as I will demonstrate.

We both will meet the principal,
and have a conversation.
Then we'll be sent home early.
Now *that's* cooperation!

You just need two to do it;
it can't be done with one.
So find a friend and give it a try—
cooperation's fun!

Special Thanks to George and Abe

To Washington and Lincoln,
two leaders of our nation,
I offer up this poem
in humble dedication.

When their birthdays come around,
I'll lead the celebration
to send these two amazing men
my thanks and admiration.

Let's give Old George and Honest Abe
a thundering ovation
for my *favorite* kind of day at school—
vacation.

My Brain Stayed Home

My brain stayed home from school today—
I left it in my bed.
It needed time to be alone,
instead of in my head.

I thought my mind could use some time
to watch TV and play.
I figured I could get along
without it for the day.

But I discovered, very soon,
what mindlessness is like.
I missed my bus, then tried to ride,
but couldn't find my bike.

All day I seemed bewildered—
forgetting stuff I knew.
Even doing easy math,
I didn't have a clue.

I failed a simple spelling test
before we went to art.
I'm pretty sure that yesterday
I knew those words by heart.

I couldn't pick a topic
when it was time for writing.
I simply was a knucklehead
when choosing or deciding.

My teacher could have yelled at me.
Instead her words were kind.
She said, "Come back tomorrow, please,
and bring your brilliant mind."

My Class Has Got a Know-It-All

My class has got a know-it-all:
the kind who likes to tell
the proper way to sit and walk
and count and speak and spell.

My class has got a know-it-all:
the kind who always knows
the stuff that happened yesterdays
or even long-agos.

She's constantly correcting me
if I'm a little wrong,
like when I shared my bug report
or when I sang a song.

You wonder why a rooster crows?
Exactly how a flower grows?
Who invented radios?
Or even if a glowworm glows?
She knows.

You ask her why the sky is blue?
How my paper airplane flew?
If a fact is false or true?
Or when our book report is due?
She knows that too.

You might think I'd be angry with
this smarty-panty creature.
But someday I will be like her...
I'm going to be a teacher.

THANKS FOR SADDLIN' UP, BUCKEROOS!

Ted

Priya

Ali

Olivia

Emma

Mariah

Louise

Sam

Ben

Gianna

Lindsey

Luke

Kyle

Anthony

Grace

Brianna

Laurel

Alexa

Nate

Aparna

Brady

Zimraan

Ted Scheu (That Poetry Guy)

Ted wears four hats comfortably and happily: The first, of course that of husband and father—to an amazing wife, and two awesome kids. Then, with his poet's hat firmly in place, Ted loves to spend his writing moments (mostly in the summer and winter) reliving his childhood and his teacherhood writing bouncy rhyming verses—like these. Ted wears his teacher hat equally proudly (mostly in the fall and spring) as he crisscrosses the globe (mostly in the NE of the US) teaching kids and teachers the magical gifts of poetry—making us all better writers! When he's not wearing one of those hats, he's probably got his bike helmet on, near his home in Middlebury, VT. Ted's poems are published widely in anthologies in the US (Philomel, Scholastic, and Meadowbrook Press), in the UK (Macmillan, Scholastic, and Hodder), and in his own collections, "I Froze My Mother," "I Tickled My Teachers," "I Threw My Brother Out," "Now I Know My ZBCs," and "Getting The Best of Me"—all from Young Poets' Press. Learn much more about Ted at his web site: **www.poetryguy.com**.

Peter Lourie

Pete is an adventurer, photographer and teacher, and, as if that's not enough, he is also a celebrated children's author. In his many award-winning books, Pete takes us to some of the most remote and rugged regions of the world including the Amazon, the Arctic, and everywhere wild in between. He just got back from somewhere 'in between'—working at high altitude in Cuzco, Peru, on a new book for kids. He also makes tons of visits to schools around the world each year—helping kids (and teachers) get excited about writing, reading and adventuring. Learn more about him at his web site **www.peterlourie.com**. When he's not traveling, Pete lives happily in Weybridge, Vermont.

Winslow Colwell

Winslow Colwell is a true man for all seasons, who also happens to be a marvelous designer of books, kites, and pretty much all things designable, printable, and buildable—many of which may be found at his web site at **www.wcolwell.com**. When he's not using his magical powers to design things like this book, he loves to read, play guitar, and try to figure out the rules to his daughter's favorite TV show, "The Voice." Win lives in East Middlebury, Vermont with his wife, daughter, three cats, and his astonishingly energetic nonagenarian father.

NEED MORE COPIES OF SOMEDAY I'LL BE A TEACHER FOR YOUR FAVORITE TEACHERS, COLLEAGUES, CLASSMATES AND FAMILY?

For super-speedy delivery, go to Ted's web site at **www.poetryguy.com** and push "Ted's Books" or "Buy!" links at the bottom of the home page, and you will be zoomed right to a list of the books, and then on to Amazon.com.

Thanks!